The Little Book of Hitchin

Pamela Shields

First Published 2008
Shoestring Publications
139 Heathfield Road
Hitchin Herts SG5 1TD
Pamela.shields@ntlworld.com

Text © Pamela Shields
Photographs© Marac and Hanae Kolodzinski
www.marack.net

ISBN 978-0-9560821-0-7

Printed by Hartham Press, Bury Mead Road Hitchin Hertfordshire SG5 1RT

Our Thanks to

Revd. Ann Pollington, St. Ippollitts Church, Benslow Music Trust, Benslow Nursing Home, David Kann Associates, David Hodges, Curator, Hitchin Museum, Hitchin Girls School, Hitchin Historical Society; Bridget and David Howlett, Pauline Humphries, Audrey Stewart, Kirk @ Market Theatre, Mavis and David Bell, Messrs John Shilcock, Michael Clark www.tewinorchard.co.uk, Pam and Peter Green and Revd. Andrew Kleissner of Christ Church Ipswich, Oliver @ Offley Place, Sid Porteous @ Hitchin Priory, Sir Simon Bowes-Lyon, The Bury, St. Paul's Walden, Steve Matthews @ Parc Computers, Hermitage Road, Sue Ryder Care Stagenhoe Park, Zoe and Alec Hunter, Cadwell Farm Ickleford and many many others.

Pamela has lived in Hitchin eleven years. She has a degree in art history and once taught in Welsh comprehensive zoos, sorry, schools. After moving to London where she lived for twenty years she transferred her highly suspect teaching skills to The British Council until the day she chucked the job, the mortgage and the kids (don't tut – they were quite old) and wandered alone through France, Belgium, Oz and America. When she came back two years later she enrolled on a post graduate course in journalism and has written for magazines ever since. She has published *Islington: The First 2000 Years*, *Essential Islington: From Boadicea to Blair*; *Hertfordshire A~Z*; *The Private Lives of Hertfordshire Writers* and is now head butting publishers to take *Hertfordshire: Secrets and Spies*. Chair of Hitchin U3A, she runs groups in French conversation - she can't speak French but likes talking - and history. The book is dedicated to her long suffering sons Jeff and Steve.

Marac, who was born in Hitchin, has travelled all over the world and ended up where he began. He and his wife **Hanae** met in Japan where Marac lived for ten years. It's now Hanae's turn to experience Marac's culture. Although she is a huge fan of Town Fryer fish and chips she is less impressed with the fact we do not remove our shoes at the front door. The pair met through a shared love of photography for which they have won many competitions. It's is their ambition to translate *The Little Book of Hitchin* into Japanese and sell it in Hanae's home town of Funabashi Chiba because Japan is very interested in English history. Marac & Hanae dedicate the photography in this book to his children, Izaak, Claude & Yoko, and Hanae's Mother Etsuko.

A Homage to Hitchin

This quirky little book about a quirky little town introduces Hitchin to: the newly arrived keen to know about the area; visitors who want to get the most out of their time here (the beauty of Hitchin is that it's walkable) and tourists with time to mooch. For proper history you need to read Hitchin Historical Society publications. Although Londoners dismiss Hitchin as the sticks it is in fact a town to be reckoned with and ought, by right, to be groaning under Blue Plaques. Hitchin Market is the largest open market in the Home Counties. This is where King Offa of the famous Dyke died. Bob Hope's family came from here - as did that of Anthony Hope Hawkins, author of *The Prisoner of Zenda*. This is where little Joe Lister of anti-septic fame started school and ended up a Lord. Sir Frank Whittle, world famous inventor of the jet engine lived here for a while and when Sir Henry Wood of Proms fame died here a train was chartered to bring mourners from London. The first chap to translate Homer came from Hitchin and George Orwell shopped in Brooker's. After the tragedy of the town's vandalisation in the 60s and 70s people breathe a sigh of gratitude for slitty eyed campaigning groups such as The Hitchin Society, Hitchin Historical Society and Keep Hitchin Special who gather under the Hitchin Forum umbrella to protect the town's heritage.

Hunting The Hiz

How lucky Hitchin is to have the river Hiz, although, it is, in the main, a sad old thing apart from of course the lovely bit in front of St. Mary's. Opinions vary on what replaced the stone fountain. Some mourn its loss saying the present fountain resembles nothing more than a burst water main, some think it an improvement, others that a water feature is not appropriate in a river, some have not even noticed the fountain has gone. Many more are completely indifferent. Such is life. If this were in France, perhaps even in Hitchin's twin town of Nuits Saint George say, the Hiz would be revered. Without it there would be no Hitchin (incidentally today's spelling first appeared in 1618). As folk need clean drinking water, a bunch of ancient Brits settled on its banks and still do on fine days. The Hiz, about ten miles long, starts in Charlton, runs on to Biggleswade where it joins the Ivel, carries on through Bedfordshire where it joins the Great Ouse, then flows into the sea at The Wash near King's Lynn. To see how Hitchin once looked with a river running through it visit Priory Gardens. Its demise probably began when Frederick Seebohm gave part of his back garden to the town and the Hiz went under tarmac to build Hermitage Road. You come across the Hiz, sometimes quite unexpectedly, all over the place including in Charlton beside the Windmill pub; as a culvert under Bridge Street; in Portmill Lane; in Sainsbury's and Iceland's car parks and various places along Grove Road. We need a new group: Friends of The Hiz. Indeed, we may already have one.

The Hiz: The Old Fountain

King OFFA
Hitchin's First Claim to Fame.

How many towns have a church built by a king? Hitchin does. Originally dedicated to St Andrew, it's now St.Mary's. Offa also built St. Alban's Abbey to honour Albanus, the first Christian martyr in northern Europe. Matthew Paris the historian-monk of St Albans who put on record that Offa lived in Offley until 'he was called to his rest' was disgusted the Abbey had not looked after its founder's body (no-one knows what happened to him). Why did Offa come to Hitchin? Because his enemy Beonred, who was holding a Great Council in nearby Benington, had grabbed Mercia (all land south of the Humber). Offa, who had a stronger claim to the throne, was having none of it. One ancestor, Offa, was king of the Angles another was Penda, King of Mercia. Offa gathered his men at Hitchin and defeated Beonred at Offa's Ley (lea/meadow). Offley Place, a lovely manor house (first built in the 1600s) is probably on the site of his palace. When Offa ruled between the Trent in the north to Kent in the south, from the Welsh border to East Anglia he was officially recognised by the Pope as *Rex Anglorum* King of the English and Hitchin became a Royal Manor. Because he was trading with France, Offa introduced the penny, with the same silver content as coins in France, as the monetary unit of England, the first English king to put his image on a coin. In 1923 one was found on a track between Hitchin and Offley bearing the inscription 'OFFA REX'. Offa's laws were so sound Alfred the Great adapted them and Offa was mentioned by his biographer: *'…Offa…had a great dyke built between Wales and Mercia from sea to sea'.* Started in 785 it's still traceable from the Wye valley to Wrexham.

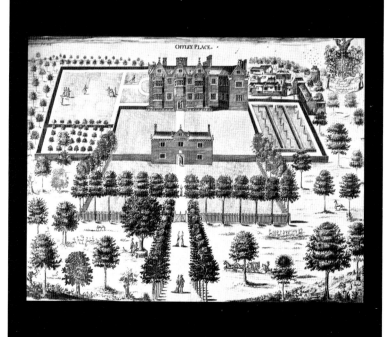

Offley Place: Date unknown

St. Mary's Church
The Grand Old Lady of Hitchin

King Offa built his large church not long before he died. Is this where he planned to be buried? Matthew Paris, the monk historian at St. Alban's Abbey said Offa was buried in a chapel on the banks of the Ouse. The Hiz is a tributary of the Ouse. Nowhere on the Ouse was there a chapel grand enough to house the body of a King. The church he built certainly was. Described in the Domesday Book as the monasterium of Hitchin, at the time of the Great Survey the church, along with the manor, belonged to the Crown. The church dedicated to St. Andrew was still called that in 1521. It's strange that it transmuted into St. Mary's considering that in 1541 Henry V111's England was C of E. Church Registers go back to 1562. The tower has what look like recycled Roman bricks; the nave dates from the 1100s the tower from the 1200s the windows from the 1400s. After the Dissolution Henry VIII gave St. Mary's and St. Ippollitts church to Trinity College, Cambridge. St. Mary's is where: John Bunyan's sister was christened; Robert Hinde is buried; Charles Lamb's grandparents were married and his mother was christened; the funeral service of Sir Henry Wood was held. There are monuments to the Delmé Radcliffe family who lived in the Priory for 400 years and to the de Kendale family who held the manor for the Crown including Robert de Kendale who fought at Crecy. The effigy of Bernard de Baliol Lord of Hitchin manor is on the window cill. One of his descendants became king of Scotland, another established Balliol College Oxford. Simon Jenkins of *The Times* said in *England's Thousand Best Churches* St. Mary's is *'the largest and jolliest…in Hertfordshire'*.

St Mary's Church Hitchin

King Canute and Earl Tovi

What is a photograph of Waltham Abbey doing in a book about Hitchin? Because Hitchin paid for it. In 1016, after his battle for the most prosperous country in Europe, Canute is King. Although his kingdom included Denmark, Sweden and Norway he went native and became more English than the English. He rewarded his standard bearer Earl Tovi - second to him in rank - by giving him Hitchin and Waltham. Canute's standard with a black raven carried into battle was believed to possess magic qualities. If he was going to win, it opened its beak and flapped its wings. If he was to be defeated, it did not stir. There was nothing in Waltham, but Hitchin was definitely worth having. Sheep meant wool for export and barley for London breweries made the town wealthy. Tovi used Hitchin revenues to found Waltham church which he built to receive the True Cross of Christ. Canute's son HarthaCnut died while guest of honour at Tovi's marriage in Lambeth. When Tovi died and his son squandered his inheritance, Hitchin reverted to the Crown. Edward the Confessor gave it to Earl Harold Godwinson who succeeded him as Harold 11. In 1066 Harold took Tovi's Cross from Waltham into the Battle of Hastings. We all know how that ended. William 1 declared himself King of England. Edith Swan Neck who bore Harold six children buried him behind the High Altar in Waltham. A stone, covered in flowers on the anniversary of his death, marks the site. William 11 stripped the church of valuables for his church in Caen. The Abbey's 100,000 visitors a year include many from Caen. The remains of Tovi's church are under the present one which became an abbey in 1184. Tovi's Cross at Waltham Abbey is not to be confused with Waltham Cross built to honour Eleanor of Castile.

Waltham Abbey: King Harold

The Baliol Family

The Domesday Book lists Hiz, the second-largest town in Hertfordshire, as a Royal Manor. If Offa had not founded St Alban's Abbey it would have been the largest. William 11 gave Hitchin to Guy from Bailleul (in Picardy) who came over to England with his father. When Bernard de Balliol (probably Guy's son) attended a Chapter of the Order of the Temple in Paris in 1147 and plans were put in action for The Second Crusade he gave land at Deneslai to the Order to build a Preceptory. The most important in South-East England this is where the Templars held their National Chapters (AGMs). Bernard joined the second Crusade in 1160. His effigy, one of the earliest in England, on the window cill in St Mary's, originally showed armour, chainmail, a sword and a shield. His legs are crossed to show he went on Crusade. To see its like, one needs to visit Temple Church in London. Made in 1162 when he returned from Crusade the effigy was on his tomb in the chapel at Temple Dinsley until the Dissolution of the monasteries. A fragment of the foot was found in the grounds in 1885. Skeletons, a chalice, a grave and 13th-century floor tiles were also found. The Princess Helena College is now on the site. Although he was a Crusader Knight, he did not join the fraternity of Templars. His descendant John de Baliol founded Balliol College in 1263. Another John de Baliol, became King of the Scots. When Edward 1, Hammer of the Scots, defeated John de Baliol at Berwick he took the Stone of Scone on which all Scottish kings were crowned to Westminster Abbey where all English Kings were crowned. When Baliol was sent back to Bailleul where his ancestors came from, Hitchin reverted to the Crown.

St Mary's Church: the Effigy

The Knights Templars

St Ippolitts Church, founded in 1087 by William the Conqueror's niece Judith, Prioress of Elstow Abbey, Bedfordshire is dedicated to Hippolytus (French do not aspirate hence 'ippo) patron saint of horses. One of only two in the UK dedicated to him, the other is in Dorset. Before going on Crusade it's said that the Templars brought their horses to the altar to be blessed. The blessing of horses has recently been revived. Crosses carved into a pillar are said to have been cut by them (it might then have been on the outside). If you can't find them imagine you are on a horse. When the Muslims won Jerusalem the Templars days were numbered. No longer needed, Philip the Fair destroyed the Order in France and asked Edward 11 to follow suit. The Preceptory must have been important. Not only were Chapters of the Order held here Temple Dinsley was given as the scene of more than one of the crimes alleged against the Templars. Edward reluctantly followed a Papal Bull and issued orders for their arrest. Two were sent to the Tower of London, four to the dungeons of Hertford Castle. Edward 111, convinced the Templars had buried treasure at Temple Dinsley set up a Royal Commission: "To inquire touching concealed goods of the Templars in the County of, Hertfordshire". Nothing was found. Nothing remains above ground of the preceptory which was grabbed by Henry V111. A mansion was built on the site. Two wings are by Edwin Lutyens for the Fenwick (department store) family. In 1915 the house was bought by Douglas Vickers of armaments fame. He sold it to the Countess of Caernarfon. She sold it in 1935 to the Princess Helena College for Girls (Helena was the third daughter of Queen Victoria). The building is Listed.

St. Ippollitts Church: Interior

The Priory

The Grade 1 Listed Priory was founded in 1317 when Edward 11 gave land to the Carmelites to build a convent and church dedicated to the Virgin Mary. He did not however give them the money needed to survive. The White Friars were mendicant monks, beggars, who relied on the good folk of Hitchin to help them out. They were here over two hundred years until 1539 when Henry V111 closed the monasteries and grabbed all church lands and assets. He had a survey done before selling The Priory. The estate included a mansion, cloister, church, hall, prior's lodging, chambers for the brothers, kitchen and barns. Properties in Bridge Street were leased out with the convent garden. Seven years later the estate was bought by the Radcliffe family who lived here for over four hundred years. One of them laid out the Park in the 1720s; another rebuilt the mansion in the 1770s. In 1802 a Radcliffe married into the Delmé family. They owned it until 1965 when twenty-two year old Millicent Delmé Radcliffe sold it to Herts County Council who used it for education. Locals still remember Millicent's wedding procession through the town from St Mary's to the Priory. The Council sold the building to National Mutual Life in 1983 later absorbed into GELife. The view from the house was unrestricted for three miles as far as Gosmore until the 1980s when the new by pass (Park Way) bisected the priory grounds. The present house, which still, miraculously, incorporates part of the old convent built by the White Friars, is now leased to the Chartridge Conference Company.

Hitchin Priory

The New Biggin
Is Now Very Old Indeed

The Biggin is a little miracle. It managed to survive the 1960s as buildings nearby were bulldozed. As for the strange name, there are many 'New Biggins' (new buildings) all over the UK. Built of timber, plaster and brick today it consists of four tiny wings with tiny rooms, a tiny courtyard and a tiny cloister – dinky is the word - but was originally part of a far larger complex of ecclesiastical buildings. In 1361 Edward de Kendale., Lord of Hitchin Manor, founded the priory of St. Saviour, New Bigging for the Gilbertine Order. His effigy is in St.Mary's. Edward who died in 1373 was succeeded by his son Edward who survived his father by two years after which Hitchin reverted to Crown. When Henry V111 grabbed all land owned by religious Orders it was bought by a local man, William Croocar who left it to his sons. 1585 is cut into panelling with initials that may be those of William Croocar Jnr. The Croocar family sold 'The Byggin' to Robert Snagge who pulled most of it down and built the present building in the late 1500s. From 1635 the Biggin was owned by Joseph Kempe who opened it as a boarding school. This had a good reputation and pupils came from all over England. As Kempe left The Biggin to support 'ten auncient or middle aged women' it was home to 'Kempe's Widows' until 1908 when the Trustees handed it over to Hitchin United Charities. In 1958 The Biggin was altered to its present arrangement for twelve residents each to have bed-sitting room, bathroom and kitchen. Today Messrs John Shilcock of Hitchin manage The Biggin for Hitchin United Charities. As they are not considered suitable for older people the units are rented by the Education Authority for teachers.

The Biggin: The Cloisters

The Wonderfully Wicked
And Wickedly Wonderful
Mrs Perrers

Edward 111 gave Hitchin to his mistress Alice Perrers for life. With its fair, water mills and revenue from the market it was well worth having. The couple probably visited the town together. The powerful, notorious, twice married Alice was lady in waiting to Edward's wife. It was rumoured that Alice, alone with the king at his death, stripped rings from his fingers. There is also another delicious rumour that to atone for her wickedness, paid for the building of St Andrew's in Essex which locals called Whore-Church. When horns were added to embellish her legend it, and the surrounding area, became known as Horn Church. Alice had, so it's said, a deep, mesmerising seductive voice. Ambitious, unscrupulous, indiscreet, shameless, impudent, harlot and greedy are some of the nicer things said about her. Who was she? She told so many lies and her reluctance to name any of her relatives means that it is impossible to know. She said she was the daughter of Hertfordshire gentry but was probably the daughter of a thatcher who got her name Perrers from her first husband, a chap of low birth. Somehow she wangled her way into court and managed to nab her second husband William of Windsor but set her sights much higher. She and Edward had four children. When he gave her the jewels and robes of his dead Queen Philippa, Alice, in a chariot bearing the logo 'Lady of the Sun' paraded through London wearing them. Alice only owned Hitchin for a year. In 1376 The Good Parliament took it from her for 'performing illegal acts' and banished her from the royal household. Royal auditors came to Hitchin to see how much it was worth and took as much as they could to pay her debts.

Hitchin Market: 2008

The First Man to Translate Homer
Is Still Not in Westminster Abbey
A Pox on All Their Houses.

The poet Charles Cowden Clarke often spoke of the night he and John Keats read George Chapman's translation of Homer. At dawn Keats went home and wrote *'On First Looking Into Chapman's Homer'* as a tribute. Chapman will always be remembered for Homer's adventures of Odysseus, the Greek warrior, as he tried to get home after the Trojan War. The world's first translator of Homer, the blind Greek poet, said he was inspired by Homer's ghost which he saw in Hitchin. Born and brought up in Tilehouse Street (now Lower Tilehouse Street) Chapman gave more words to the English language than any other writer including Shakespeare. A close friend of Ben Jonson and Walter Raleigh, he is said to be the rival poet in Shakespeare's Sonnets. Among his contemporaries, Edmund Spencer, Philip Henslowe, Christopher Marlowe, Inigo Jones and Francis Bacon, he is the only genius not publicly honoured. As he said: '…Homer no patron found nor Chapman friend'. Chapman wrote *An Epic Poem about Guiana* predicting a future English empire. When he made fun of the Scots in *Eastward Ho!* he was jailed. Chapman finished Christopher Marlowe's *Hero and Leander* when Marlowe was murdered. In 1616 the *Iliad* and *Odyssey* appeared in *The Whole Works of Homer*. Ben Jonson's first edition of *The Iliad* is in the British Library. Coleridge also owned a first edition, as did William Wordsworth and Charles Lamb who kissed his copy before opening it. Chapman's twelve books are in the Bodleian Library. The films *Cold Mountain* and *O Brother, Where Art Thou?* are based on Odysseus. Chapman who died in poverty is buried in St Giles in the Fields. Jonson and Keats who revered him have memorials in Westminster Abbey. Chapman does not.

The Chapman House: Lower Tilehouse Street

John Bunyan

Bunyan's *Pilgrim's Progress* has never been out of print. The only portrait Bunyan had painted of him while he was alive was found in Codicote (now in the National Portrait Gallery). Although his sister was baptised at St Mary's, the vicar banned Bunyan from preaching in town. He met followers in what is now known as Bunyan's Dell in Wain Wood and, so it's thought, in the barn at Maydencroft Manor in Gosmore. He was so attractive to women, enemies accused him of having an affair with Agnes Beaumont. Her father hated Bunyan so forbade Agnes to attend his meetings warning if she went against him she would be disinherited. The only way she could get to a meeting was to ride pillion behind a man on his horse - something frowned upon. One evening, she went to her brother's to go with him and his wife to hear Bunyan but was let down by a family friend who had offered her a lift. Seeing Bunyan, her brother asked if Agnes could share his horse. Her father saw them together and locked her out. When she was allowed home her father dropped dead within three days. Revd. Lane, a clergyman spread rumours about Agnes and Bunyan. Also, a local solicitor, Mr Farrow, asked Agnes to marry him. When she turned him down he too, spread rumours saying in order not to lose her inheritance she murdered her father and Bunyan got the poison. A post mortem was ordered but neither Farrow nor Lane's evidence held up in court. The coroner concluded John Beaumont died of natural causes. Agnes is buried in an unmarked grave near John Wilson, the first pastor of Upper Tilehouse Street Baptist chapel which Bunyan founded in 1669. Wilson and Bunyan were in prison together for refusing to take the oath of allegiance to the Church of England.

The Baptist Church: Upper Tilehouse Street

The Body Snatchers

Life was far more interesting in the old days when you could bury Great Aunt Maud any old where. Take Richard Tristram for example, a solicitor from Portmill Lane. He and Henry Trigg from High Street Stevenage were passing St. Mary's churchyard one night when they saw body snatchers digging up the dearly departed to sell to medical students (other sources say they saw the sexton digging up old bones to make room for new). In 1828 when the corpse of newly buried twenty-one year old Elizabeth Whitehead was stolen, gates and railings were put around the churchyard (still there in 1938). Horrified this might happen to them Richard and Henry left instructions in their wills on how they should be buried. Tristram ordered his executors buy land for his interment within the sound of running water. His son bought a field near Folly Brook, White Hill, St. Ippollitts. The grave, once railed off, is near the Oakfield housing estate near the A602 going out of Hitchin near Kingshott School. Until it was sold, rent for the field went to Skynner's Almshouses in Bancroft. As for Henry Trigg he ordered his coffin be put in the rafters of his barn. When he died in 1724 his brother, Reverend Thomas Trigg, followed instructions. Fifty years later, Henry's niece left money for her uncle to be given a decent burial. Was he? Apparently not. In 1831 when the old barn belonged to the Castle Inn the landlord inspected the coffin and said Henry was still there. In 1906 East Hertfordshire Archaeological Society confirmed a skeleton was inside. In 1927 a carpenter made a new coffin. Today, the barn is owned by the Nat West Bank. Locals say the coffin is still in the rafters. If so, is Henry?

St. Mary's Churchyard

By George
It's the 4th of July

The George in Bucklersbury is a tribute to George Washington, President of the USA. Why? Legend has it that William Gordon, a local chap, was his secretary. He wasn't. However, he was Chaplain to the American Congress, started the 4 July celebrations and wrote the first eye witness account of the War of Independence. The myth probably started when Gordon moved into Mount Vernon, Washington's home. With open access to his papers he began to write the history of the War. The men, near in age, had Hertfordshire in common, Washington's grandfather came from Tring. Gordon, a controversial, outspoken, non-conformist Minister, married a girl from Cockernhoe. Baptised in Back Street (now Queen Street) Congregational Chapel, he came home often to worship. In the 1960s when the chapel was demolished some of the bones found were buried in a common grave the rest were left in situ under an office car park. When the office block was demolished an archaeological excavation was carried out by the Heritage Network following the correct procedure for the exhumation of bodies. Rallying to America's cause Gordon took up a post in Boston. Although he begged the rebels not to go through with the famous 'Tea Party' Britain found him guilty of treason in absentia. On the first anniversary of Independence, Gordon celebrated it in a sermon. Harvard, Yale and Princeton awarded him an MA. When he refused American citizenship, said slavery was unconstitutional and put forward plans for Emancipation he was dismissed from Congress. He came back to write: *The History of the Rise Progress and Establishment of the Independence of the United States of America including an Account of the Late War and of the Thirteen Colonies from their Origin to that Period.* His last Ministry was at Christ Church Ipswich where he died in 1807.

The George Inn: Bucklersbury

The Schoolmaster's Secret

When Eugene Aram, a highly respected Hitchin teacher moved away no-one thought any more about him until the day he was arrested for murder. But for a case of mistaken identity - of a corpse - he would never have been traced. In 1758, in Yorkshire, a labourer digging for stone unearthed a skeleton. People assumed it was Daniel Clark who had suddenly left town thirteen years earlier after conning locals out of their valuables. Because Clark was last seen with Richard Houseman and Eugene Aram they were arrested. Cleared of all charges Aram left town. His abandoned wife told the police before Clark disappeared he was in her house with Houseman and her husband. When the police questioned Houseman he asked where the skeleton was found. On being told said it could be 'no more Dan Clark…than it is mine' with such certainty he aroused suspicion. Questioned again he revealed that Clark was killed miles away from where the skeleton was found. Accused of Clark's murder he said although he was there when he died it was Aram who struck the fatal blow. Houseman was acquitted, Aram, found guilty, confessed. Writers fell over themselves to tell his story. Thomas Hood wrote *The Dream of Eugene Aram*. Charles Dickens raved over Lord Lytton's best selling novel *Eugene Aram*. Researching for it Lytton of Knebworth House questioned everyone in Hitchin who remembered Aram. Why was their imagination roused? Not only did Aram never say why he killed Clark he left a self-published book in his cell: *A Comparative Lexicon of the English, Latin, Greek, Hebrew and Celtic Languages*. During his years on the run Aram had taught himself Latin and Greek. He was the first to say that all European languages originate from the Celtic language. In 1831 he was proved right.

Aram Alley

A Lovable Eccentric

Robert Hinde, a retired, eccentric, army captain, was perhaps the first war gamer. He spent his days reconstructing battles. He transformed his home Hunsdon House into Preston Castle with turrets, battlements, portcullises, ramparts and fortifications; raised earthworks, dug trenches and installed cannons on his front lawn. On the anniversary of famous battles he put his servant Pilgrim on horseback as Herald while he rode behind followed by his six sons, eleven daughters and offspring of servants and villagers all dressed in scarlet uniforms with blue sashes wearing beaver hats (nicknamed The Preston Light Dragoons) into Market Square. The old man on horseback, a military figure in full army regalia covered in ribbons and medals blowing a trumpet to proclaim some long forgotten battle was a much-loved figure. There was a patriotic rendering of the national anthem before returning home where he was welcomed by a salute of guns before the drawbridge was lowered. When Laurence Sterne visited Kimpton Hoo to stay with Thomas Brand, Lord Dacre, he met Hinde who years later turned up as the lovable Uncle Toby in Sterne's novel *The Life and Opinions of Tristram Shandy, Gentleman.* Terry Brighton in *The Last Charge* the history of The Royal Regiment, The King's Own Light Dragoons said the caricature is unfair to Hinde who was an accomplished cavalry officer. Hinde published *The Discipline of the Light Horse* in 1778. The manual which covers very aspect of training and correct practice set the standards for light cavalry regiments in the British army for decades. Captain Hinde's book is in the Regimental archives. Hinde, along with his parents and seventeen children were all buried in St Mary's. There is grand memorial to them in the church. When the last Hinde died in 1855, the estate was sold off. One lot became Castle Farm.

The Market Square

A Family Tragedy

Mary Bruton and Edward Field from Hitchin got married in St Mary's. Their daughter Elizabeth was baptised there. When Elizabeth Field married John Lamb they had three children, Mary, John and Charles. Once a world famous writer, today Charles Lamb is almost forgotten. He wrote magazine pieces about the happy holidays he spent in what he called 'Hearty, homely, loving Hertfordshire'. Lamb's funny essays such as *Dissertation on a Roast Pig* hid the tragedy of his life. When he fell in love with Ann Simmons on one of his holidays in Hertfordshire his grandmother advised him never to get married or have children because there was insanity in the Lamb family. Heartbroken he followed her advice. His poem *Dream Children* is about the children he wanted with Ann. His grandmother's warning proved true. When his bosom pal Samuel Taylor Coleridge left Britain a bereft Charles, 20, became unhinged and was confined to an asylum. His sister Mary who adored him was so distraught she too went mad. She attacked and wounded their father then stabbed and killed their mother. She too was sent to an asylum. When Charles was released his brother advised him to break all ties with Mary. Instead he asked for her to be released into his care and looked after her for the rest of his life. Although he toiled as a lowly office clerk his writing talent brought him into contact with the giants of the literary world who were all devoted to him. His friends included Mary Shelley (although he disliked her husband Percy Bysshe), Lord Byron and William Wordsworth. With Mary he wrote *Children's Tales from Shakespeare* and, inspired by his hero George Chapman from Hitchin, *Children's Tales from Homer* and *The Adventures of Ulysses*.

St. Mary's Church: Interior

The Doctor Who Invented Anti-septic

Joseph Lister, whose name will forever be linked with the use of anti-septic, always knew he wanted to be a surgeon. His boyhood hobby was dissecting animals. Hitchin was known for its prestigious boarding schools such as The Isaac Brown Quaker Academy whose most famous pupil was Joseph Lister of Listerine mouthwash fame. His father, Friend Lister, was the physicist known for inventing the microscope. Joseph was the first surgeon to sterilise his surgical instruments and to use carbolic acid to sterilise cuts and wounds. Today surgery is known as pre-Lister and post-Lister. Little Joe Lister Jnr whose name one day will rank alongside those of Louis Pasteur, Alexander Fleming and Edward Jenner arrived in Hitchin age five to board at Isaac Brown's school. His cousin William Lucas lived in nearby Tilehouse Street. Friend Lucas was a wealthy brewer. In adult life Joe Lister as Lord Lister with his wife Isabella and their son often stayed with his cousin in Hitchin. Little Joe, whose relatives kept an eye on him, wrote home every week sometimes in French sometimes in Latin. As a surgeon, Lister saw half his patients die from sepsis. Knowing that fields treated with carbolic acid were free from the parasites which cause disease in cattle he tried a very weak solution of it to sterilise his surgical instruments and used it as an antiseptic in surgery. In his lifetime, he saw the death rate during and following surgery drop from 80 per cent to almost nil. Before Lister, we died of erysipelas, septicaemia, streptococcus, gangrene and tetanus. Today it's MRI. He was created Baron Lister of Lyme Regis. Isaac Brown's school closed in 1845. Today The Lord Lister Hotel is on the site.

The Lord Lister Hotel

William Ransom
and The Body Shop

Isaac Brown's Academy must have been very good for science. As well as Joseph Lister it produced the founder of Britain's first independent pharmaceutical company. William Ransom who was born in the family farmhouse in Bancroft was a school friend of Lister. Until recently when Ransom moved to new, state of the art, premises, Sainsbury customers in Bancroft could smell The Body Shop's Dewberry brewed by Ransom. Behind the plaque of 105 Bancroft, a mercifully protected fourteenth century gate house, is the fascinating story of Ransom who, at the astonishingly young age of 19, founded the Company on the farm where he was born. He grew many of the plants he needed (belladonna, henbane, foxgloves, and broom) and paid locals to pick dandelions, poppies, rosehips and elder. Men brought them on donkey carts, boxes on wheels or in sacks; women and children arrived with aprons brimming over. Elder is still used in insect repellents and ointments for bruises, sprains and chilblains. William's skills were certainly needed. Few could afford doctors. Until Joseph Lister invented antiseptic people put their faith in weird and wonderful potions. Ransom also grew lavender. In 1851, he presented a bottle of his lavender water to Queen Victoria when the royal train stopped at Hitchin. A keen archaeologist, on one of his thirty mile rambles around Hitchin, William found the skeleton of an Anglo-Saxon all 6 foot 4 of him sitting bolt upright; the ashes of a mother and child with a baby's feeding bottle; a woman's Alice band, scent bottle, coins dating from 193 AD and, amazingly, a grand, centrally heated, seven room Roman house with bathrooms. *The paint or fresco on the walls retained in places the colour as...when first put on...within seven inches of the surface [although] the land has been tilled by the plough for ages'.*

105 Bancroft: 2008

Good On Yer Emily

Emily Davies founded Britain's first women's residential college of higher education in Hitchin. Denied the opportunity of education herself, she was envious of her brother John Llewelyn Davies's success at Cambridge. His barrister son, her nephew, Arthur Llewellyn Davies, who lived in Berkhamsted, was the father of Peter, George, John, Michael and Nicholas who inspired J.M.Barrie's *Peter Pan*. Arthur loathed Barrie saying he gave him the creeps. Emily would see Arthur, his wife Sylvia - the daughter of George du Maurier who wrote *Trilby* - and George and Michael die young. Arthur and Sylvia died from cancer, George died in WW1, and Michael committed suicide. Peter also committed suicide in the 1960s. Barrie's obsession with Sylvia was spookily similar to that of Svengali and Trilby. Emily, of enormous support to Elizabeth Garrett in her attempt to become a doctor, dedicated her life getting women into higher education. When she petitioned the University of London to accept women and was turned down yet again she decided to start her own College for Women in Benslow House. This was fine for a while but the place her students needed to be to compete with men was Cambridge so Emily managed to raise £7,000 to build a college near Girton. Her friend the novelist George Eliot sent a donation. Some locals were not sorry to see her avant-garde students leave. Not only did they swim in Queen Street open air pool they played cricket and tennis and dressed as men to act in Shakespeare. One critic called the college 'that infidel place'. Although Emily's students passed the Tripos exam the University of Cambridge refused to award them degrees. Women students at Girton were not admitted to full membership of the University until 1948. Benslow House is now a private nursing home.

Benslow Nursing Home

Mr Butterfield Comes to Town

William Butterfield was one of nine children. Apprenticed to a builder, he went on to become one of Britain's most famous, most prestigious, most highly paid of Victorian Gothic architects and won the Royal Institute of British Architects (RIBA) Gold Medal. Butterfield's gothic masterpiece is All Saints in Margaret Street, London. The chapel he designed at Keble College Oxford has a wonderful interior decorated with coloured tiles and mosaics. He also designed Merton College; Balliol College Chapel Oxford; Tyntesfield near Bristol; Milton Ernest Hall and its watermill in Bedfordshire for the Stacey family, to whom he was related by marriage. When the railway came to Hitchin the surrounding area was quickly developed. It had many houses but no church so Reverend George Gainsford Senior asked Butterfield to design Holy Saviour Church in Radcliffe Road. Butterfield's choice of red brick was not for reasons of economy. He made the brick work patterns and diaper work the main feature because he wanted to give dignity to brick. He designed everything, hinges, light fittings and heating. He disapproved of hassocks, which he said people tripped over, so designed a fold-out kneeling board. The interior today is much darker than Butterfield intended. Like Christopher Wren he preferred his churches to be light so used plain glass and did not design the stained glass windows. They were added later as were the Stations of the Cross. Holy Saviour is worth a visit at any time but especially during December to see the impressive display of decorated Christmas trees during Hitchin's annual Christmas Tree Festival.

Holy Saviour Church: Radcliffe Road

The Wandering Minstrel
In Stagenhoe Park

The almighty Mikado, Yum Yum, Nanki-Poo, Ko-Ko and Pooh-Bah were all born near Hitchin when Sir Arthur Sullivan, famous composer of the comic Savoy operas he created with W. S. Gilbert, rented Stagenhoe Park near St Paul's Walden (now a Sue Ryder Care Centre). He paid £189 p.a (£12,000) rent, which included valet, chef and three housemaids. Built in 1737 Stagenhoe had 33 bedrooms and nine acres. In the 1880s, there was a huge interest in Japanese fashion and it was here that Sir Arthur wrote his ninth opera *The Mikado*. When the show was first performed in 1885 it set a London box office record that lasted 33 years. The production was very Japanese. Gilbert employed geishas to teach the actresses how to move and to use fans. He bought real Japanese kimonos for the cast and asked the principals to shave their eyebrows and paint Japanese ones half way up their foreheads. Sullivan invited the whole D'Oyly Carte Opera Company for weekends. It's said that after performing in London he took the midnight train which terminated at Hatfield, made the driver an offer he couldn't refuse and bribed him to take the train on to Hitchin paying him £1 per mile. Safely back in Hitchin he was still some way from home, so presumably his man and coach would be waiting for him. As his father was bandmaster at the Royal Military College, Sandhurst by the time he was eight, Arthur could play every instrument in the band. Charles Dickens was a huge admirer of Sullivan and often told him so. Sullivan expected to be buried with his parents and brother in Brompton Cemetery but his biggest fan, Queen Victoria, ordered that after a state funeral he be laid to rest in St. Paul's.

Stagenhoe Park

The Prisoner of Zenda
And The Hawkins of Hitchin

Anthony Hope Hawkins, barrister turned novelist, pseudonym Anthony Hope, was a member of the Hawkins of Hitchin family. He gave the English language a new word, Ruritania, when he published *The Prisoner of Zenda*. Now a classic, it was so successful he abandoned his legal career to write full time. Anthony Hope was England's answer to Alexandre Dumas. *The Prisoner of Zenda* which rivalled sales of *The Count of Monte Cristo* and *The Man in the Iron Mask* was turned into plays, musicals and films. Being French, Dumas was given a state funeral. Being English, we have forgotten all about Anthony Hope Hawkins. When Anthony visited his relatives in Hitchin – he mentions the town in his memoirs - he stayed in Bancroft where his father Reverend Edward Hawkins and his uncle John were brought up. His grandmother moved into the house with her two sons when her husband Dr Frederick Hawkins died. John was a partner in Hawkins Solicitors, Portmill Lane. The second oldest (1591) firm of solicitors in England which is still in the old Queen Anne building has in its archives the Great Seals of Elizabeth 1, James 1 and Charles 11. The Hawkins family tree has many branches but the Frederick Hawkins who built Hitchin's first hospital in Bedford Road was probably Anthony's grandfather. John Hawkins helped establish the Town Hall and the Corn Exchange. Anthony Hope, who knew J.M.Barrie, was invited to the world première of *Peter Pan* at the Duke of York's theatre. Surrounded by screaming children he sat completely unmoved. Asked for his opinion on the play in the interval he said: 'Oh, for an hour of Herod!' Hope whose portrait is in the National Portrait Gallery was knighted in recognition of his contribution to British propaganda efforts during World War I.

Portmill Lane

The Queen Mother

In 1983 H.M the Queen Mother opened The Queen Mother Theatre in Hitchin, the only theatre in the UK to be named after her. When the Lady Elizabeth Bowes-Lyon lived at The Bury in St Paul's Walden her governess, Marion Wilkie of 58 Dacre Road, cycled to St Paul's Walden until her health gave out. After that Elizabeth and her younger brother David were driven to her home in a pony and trap. They also had dancing lessons in the ballroom of the Sun Hotel. Her nanny, Clara Knight, was the daughter of a local farmer. In 1926 in the Strathmore's' town house in Bruton Street, London, Clara will also be nanny to her first child the present HM Queen Elizabeth 11. In September 1900 Elizabeth Bowes-Lyon, daughter of the Earl of Strathmore, was christened in the beautiful little church All Saints, St Paul's Walden. The Earl spent much of the year at The Bury. The ninth of ten children, Lady Elizabeth was born seven years after the birth of his previous child. When the Earl finally got round to registering his daughter's birth he was fined for not registering within the legal time limit. Until she married, Lady Elizabeth spent much of her life in St. Paul's Walden and returned every summer. In 1923 King George V's son Prince Albert, the Duke of York visited St Paul's Walden to propose to Lady Elizabeth. The Duke and Duchess of York often visited The Bury as a family. There is a photo of princesses Elizabeth and Margaret taken there. It's said that as a child Lady Elizabeth had her hand read by a palmist at a local fete; 'She says I'm going to be a queen when I grow up! Isn't it silly?' In 1937 Lady Elizabeth Bowes-Lyon was crowned Queen in Westminster Abbey.

All Saint's Church: St. Paul's Walden

Thanks For The Memory

In 1907 William Hope went home to Hitchin say goodbye to his father before emigrating to America. James Hope must have felt sad. Two other sons Frank and Fred were already there. William's son, Bob Hope, wisecracked 'I left England at the age of four when I found out I couldn't be king'. James, a stonemason, worked on the Statue of Liberty in Paris (it was then shipped to New York) and the Royal Courts of Justice in the Strand. William, born and brought up in Hitchin, was, like his father, a stonemason. In 1939 Bob received a letter from Aunt Lucy of Brampton Park Road inviting him over saying his grandfather James was living with her. Hope worked the invitation into his act before boarding the *SS Normandie* for his first trip 'back home'. 'We had a great ball in the pub down in Hitchin. I invited all the relatives . . . never seen them before . . . grandfather James got up – he was 96 . . . introduced everybody, told a couple of jokes and did a little dance so you can see where my ham comes from.' He always said he inherited his sense of humour from his grandfather. As the Queen Mary drew away from Southampton two days before war was declared James shouted 'See you on my 100th'. In 1943 visiting American air bases in Hertfordshire on a morale boosting tour, Bob Hope heard that his grandfather was ill so went to Hitchin and said 'Come on grandpa, I'm going to take you on stage with me'. James died two days later. Hope attended the funeral. In the 1950s Bob hosted a party for his Hitchin relatives at the Sun Hotel and in 1982 hosted another at the Blakemore Hotel, Little Wymondley.

Brampton Park Road

Big Brother
In Hitchin

In 1936, Eric Blair, now known to the world as George Orwell, moved to nearby Wallington, *Animal Farm's* 'Willingdon'. Manor Barn is still there. When he bought an Albertine rose from Woolworth's he wrote about it in his *Tribune* column. He usually cycled into town but sometimes got a lift from his neighbour, Mr Field, when he brought cattle to Hitchin Market. Hitchin is where Orwell met up with Jack Common his closest friend. Whenever Orwell was away Jack looked after his animals and his cottage. Orwell wrote to him from Tangier telling him to use only Jeyes toilet paper in the lavatory or it would block, how to make mash for the chickens and if the chimney smoked he should go to Brookers who would advise him. It was Jack, who lived in Sandon, who found the cottage for Orwell. Many letters survive between the friends. 'Dear Jack, about Saturday. How about meeting me in Hitchin on Sat at 2 p.m. I think the best place to meet would be Woolworth's.' One day something happened which so shocked Orwell it triggered *1984*, BIG BROTHER, Winston Smith and the Thought Police. Orwell opened his door to police who confiscated his copies of *Tropic of Cancer* and *Black Spring*, written by his friend Henry Miller. Hitchin Sorting Office was opening his mail. Orwell was handed a written warning by the public prosecutor ordering him not to import banned books. Orwell said that if that could happen in Hitchin, dictators could take over England as they had in Germany, Russia and Spain. What Orwell did not know was that Big Brother had been watching him for years. MI5 had kept a secret dossier since he first wrote for *The Daily Worker*. They reported on his 'odd clothes and unorthodox views'.

Brookers

The French Connection

Claire Tomalin the acclaimed biographer who has won numerous literary prizes was a pupil at Hitchin Girls' Grammar School. At school her favourite reading included biographies. She once said we read biographies because, 'We are human beings, programmed to be curious about other human beings, and to experience something of their lives'. Her own life is the embodiment of triumph over tragedy. Her parents divorced when she was little. Her third child died when he was a month old, her fourth committed suicide and her fifth was born with spina bifida. Her first husband was killed while reporting for *The Sunday Times* from the Golan Heights during the Yom Kippur war and her mother developed Alzheimer's. Born Marguerite Delavenay to a French father and an English mother, she attended the French Lycée in London. When she was seven her parents separated. Caught up in a custody battle, she spent her childhood moving between schools. One was Hitchin Girls' School then a grammar school where she was a pupil from 1942 to 1947. She was Head Girl in 1946. At Newnham she and Sylvia Plath were taught by the same professor. Under sentence of death in France General Charles de Gaulle escaped to London to broadcast to his countrymen via the BBC. 18th June, 1940. I, *General de Gaulle, now in London, call on all French officers and men who are at present on British soil, or may be in the future, with or without their arms; I call on all engineers and skilled workmen from the armaments factories who are at present on British soil, or may be in the future, to get in touch with me. Whatever happens, the flame of the French resistance must not and shall not die'.* His right hand man at the Beeb was Claire Tomalin's father, Emile Delavenay.

Hitchin Girls School

Local Girl Done Good

Acclaimed writer Victoria Glendinning is a Hertfordshire lass through and through. Frederick Seebohm, her great grandfather, lived in The Hermitage, Bancroft (demolished in the 1920s, Clement and Jocelyne occupies part of the site). His son Hugh, her grandfather, lived in Preston. Her parents lived first in Sootfield Green near Preston where she was born before moving to Chapmore End not far from Hertford. Ms Glendinning lived at Pondside, Graveley, not far from her uncle for ten years with her second husband Terence de Vere White. Frederic Seebohm, a wealthy banker, an amateur, talented historian was devoted to Hitchin. In 1874 he gave part of his vast back garden, which stretched as far as Windmill Hill, to Hitchin to lay out Hermitage Road as a short cut to the station. Seebohm, one of the Founders of Hitchin Girls Grammar School in 1906 gave it its site on Windmill Hill. His daughters gave the rest of the hill to the people of Hitchin in 1921. Frederick Seebohm's great grand-daughter Victoria Seebohm, now Glendinning, biographer, novelist, critic, and broadcaster won the James Tait Black Memorial Prize, the Duff Cooper Prize and the Whitbread Biography Award. She was a psychiatric social worker before becoming a writer. Her first book, *A Suppressed Cry: Life and Death of a Quaker Daughter* a memoir of her great-aunt is about Frederick Seebohm's daughter Winnie, who died in the 1880s. It is now a Virago Modern Classic. Winnie, one of the first women to go to Newnham College, Cambridge, tragically died of asthma at the age of twenty-two. It was Winnie's brother Hugh, Victoria's grandfather, who built Poynders End. She and fellow writer Claire Tomalin, who went to Hitchin Girls Grammar School which Frederick Seebohm founded, are friends.

Hermitage Road

The Proms Come to Hitchin
Under Sad Circumstances

Sir Henry Wood famous all over the world for his Promenade Concerts which he began in 1895 when he was 26 died in Hitchin Hospital. The 'Proms' are now the world's biggest classical music festival. His first wife, Olga, was the daughter of a princess. When she died, he married Muriel Greatorex and moved into Apple Tree Dell, Chorleywood. Plans for their Gertrude Jekyll garden are in the Museum of Garden History in London. When the marriage ended in divorce Jessie Goldsack, his third wife, ostensibly became his nurse. She had relatives in Weston. While staying there, Sir Henry suffered a stroke and the local doctor, Doctor Skeggs, was called. During the war, when public concerts in London were cancelled and a flying bomb landed on his home, Sir Henry and the BBC Symphony Orchestra moved to Bedford. On the morning of 28 July 1944 Sir Henry rehearsed everything on the programme planned for that evening except for Beethoven's Seventh Symphony saying the orchestra was playing like a bunch of civil servants. That night, in his hotel, he became ill. Dr Skeggs scoured the area for a private nursing home but the only available bed was in Hitchin Hospital where he died. His widow, invited to stay with Dr Skeggs, arranged a grand funeral service held in St Mary's. The BBC Symphony Orchestra was conducted by Sir Adrian Boult. LNER put on a special return train for mourners from London. Sir Henry instructed his ashes be scattered on the roof of his beloved Queen's Hall but due to German bombs it no longer had one so they are in St Sepulchre's Holborn where he played the organ as a boy.

St. Mary's Church

Reginald Hine's
Life Long Love Affair
With Hitchin

In 1918, Reginald Hine, a young solicitor, begins writing about Hitchin, a town he loved, and carried on writing about it until he died. His books are a must for anyone who wants to know anything about the town. One of them lists people he calls *Hitchin Worthies* little dreaming he would become one himself. Other books include: *Hitchin Priory; The History of Hitchin; Samuel Lucas; A Short Story of St Mary's; History of Hitchin Grammar School; The Official Guide to Hitchin; The Natural History of The Hitchin Region; The Story of Methodism at Hitchin; The Story of the Sun Hotel; The Story of Hitchin Town; Confessions of an Un-Common Attorney; Hitchin Old and New; The Hitchin Countryside; Charles Lamb and His Hertfordshire*. Tall, handsome, extrovert and flamboyant, he wore velvet jackets, bow ties, green suits, pink shirts, spats and cycled with an open umbrella in the rain. His office was furnished with Queen Anne and Sheraton antiques. What few realised was that Hine fought a heroic battle against depression all his life until the day a series of upsetting incidents proved too much and he jumped in front of a train coming in to Hitchin station. Local resident Richard Whitmore has written *The Ghosts of Reginald Hine*, the definitive biography of a much loved man. Hine has a plaque on his old home 52 Wymondley Road and another on the wall of the Reginald Hine Memorial Garden in Lower Tilehouse Street.

The Reginald Hine Memorial Garden

When Len Met Sue

In 1948 when Leonard Cheshire inherited a house in Hampshire he was asked by the local hospital to take in an ex-serviceman dying of cancer. By 1952 he had opened four Homes but by then was himself ill with TB. All in all, Cheshire opened eighty Homes for the disabled including one in St John's Road Hitchin, now in Lavender Fields. This was at a time when the disabled were ignored, not included in main stream society, not talked about, brushed under the carpet, many years before anti-discrimination laws. In 1955 Leonard Cheshire, Baron Cheshire VC, national hero - one of the most famous airmen of the war the youngest Group Captain in the RAF, invited Sue Ryder to see his newly opened Home in Ampthill, Bedfordshire. Although his was a household name, she had never heard of him. When the arranged day in a freezing February came she was suffering from a kidney infection but determined to keep her appointment. On arrival she found the gates locked so, ill and cold, was about to go home but, realising these were the wrong gates, those leading on to the park, she pressed on. Although neither was to know it, each had met their soul mate. The couple talked about plans for their respective ventures, became Trustees in each other's charity and married four years later. Not content with excelling themselves during the war above and beyond the call of duty, this indomitable duo decided to sort out some of the carnage left in its wake by helping the sick, homeless and destitute in war torn Europe. What he witnessed in the war turned Leonard Cheshire into a pacifist. He dedicated the rest of his life to working for world peace and was a lifelong member of the Campaign for Nuclear Disarmament (CND).

Lavender Fields

Sue Ryder

When you pop in to a Sue Ryder charity shop do you wonder who she was? Sue Ryder was born in 1923. One of the many amazing facts about her is that she worked for Special Operations Executive (SOE), during the war. She met people of such superhuman courage and saw suffering on such a scale she vowed that when peace came she would found a living memorial, The Sue Ryder Foundation, to commemorate them. Her dogged determination spanned five decades of astonishing achievements and transformed the lives of hundreds of thousands. Hers is the story of FANY's and Bods. FANY stands for the First Aid Nursing Yeomanry. They supported Bods which stands for Bodies the nickname given to the secret agents who helped Resistance Fighters. Sue Ryder who called residents in her Homes, Bods in their honour, opened 18 Care Centres and 430 shops. She started house hunting for a holiday home for survivors from Nazi occupied countries or tortured by the Gestapo in Auschwitz and Ravensbruck. Groups travelled by rail and ferry – The Red Cross provided food along the way – to Dover where they were met. The scheme ended in 1979 when it ran out of money. In 1969 Sue Ryder bought Stagenhoe Park from the Countess of Caithness. During the war it was a maternity home for evacuees, 2000 babies were born there This was where the Queen Mother as a child played with the Bailey Hawkins children and in 1988 she opened the new wing. Sue Ryder turned it into a nursing home for the handicapped and for respite nursing care. Today it provides specialised neurological care and support for sufferers of MS, Parkinson's, motor neurone, stroke, Huntingdon's, dementia and (acquired) brain injury.

Sue Ryder Care

The Amazing Mrs GREY

Who was Jill Grey who has a Place named after her? One of the saviours of The British Schools in Queen Street, another of Hitchin's jewels. During the war, as a Women's Auxiliary Air Force (WAAF) officer Jill Shepherd, as she was then, operated telex machines on the south coast before joining the Signals Branch as a Code and Cipher (C&C) officer. The vital C&C department started three days after war was declared, the first WAAFS to go overseas were C and C officers. Involved in highly secret work Miss Shepherd was attached to Sir Winston Churchill's war cabinet and went with him to the Tunis, Yalta and Potsdam conferences to handle his secret signals traffic. After the war she married and settled in Hitchin – she said she was conceived in the Sun Hotel. Mrs Grey went to America as PA to the inventor of the jet engine, Wing Commander Sir Frank Whittle on a lecture tour when he was negotiating with American companies who wanted to use his invention. Whittle lived at 41 Bearton Green for a while. She then became interested in the history of education and began collecting artefacts, books, postcards, furniture and costumes. An acknowledged expert she was often consulted by The V&A and the BBC. In 1969 The British Schools closed. By 1975 Mrs Grey had managed to get it Listed. She opened a museum of education there in 1979 and wrote to Professor Lord Asa Briggs about it. The Lancasterian Classroom, built to accommodate 300 boys, is probably the only one left in the world. The Victorian Gallery Classroom is probably the only one of its kind left in the UK. Mrs Grey left her collection, one of the most significant and comprehensive of its kind, to North Herts District Council.

The British Schools

Power To The (Musical) People

If you want to learn to play any musical instrument, borrow one (if you are under 25) or listen to the Hitchin Symphony Orchestra – the fact a town of this size has one is very impressive - pop along to the Benslow Music Trust. In 1929 when Mary Ibberson a local musician decided to meet the needs for people who wanted to go on enjoying music after they left school she started providing good teaching to amateurs of all ages in country towns and villages. Little Benslow Hills, a house built in the 1800s, was the home of Esther Seebohm. She and Mary Ibberson, both Quakers, believed in adult education. Although Esther left the house to be used exclusively for the support of music, in 1978, due to financial difficulties, the Trustees decided to sell it for redevelopment. At the eleventh hour, a group of horrified members managed to oust the council and form a new one, Benslow Music Trust. It must have done something right because membership is now 1,500. The Arts Council which calls the Trust a 'haven for musicians' gave it a million pounds of lottery money to be spent on new architecture. The result is the magnificent Waldeck Wing complex of recital hall, practice rooms and accommodation. The Trust is now able to run residential music courses for adult amateur musicians. On offer is a varied programme of 100 short courses, ranging from early music to jazz.

Benslow Music Trust: 2008

Lavender Blue Dilly Dilly

Lavender 'palsy drops' were used in England in the 1200s for 'disorders of the head and nerves' and lavender is still used in homeopathy. Its oil, one of few which can be applied directly on to the skin, is aid to raise the spirits. As early as 1568 Hitchin was recorded as a lavender growing area. 'Lavender! Sweet lavender!' was one of the famous Cries of London. In the 1800s when acres of the stuff was planted Hitchin became a tourist attraction. The scent could be smelled miles away. To get a sense of what it was like visit Grasse in Provence. Every five years when plants were dug up and burnt another lovely aroma blew across town. Harry Perks had a stab at growing lavender when he opened his pharmacy in 1760. His son Edward was more successful in 1823 and his son Sam even more so in 1840. When Perks joined Charles Llewelyn Hitchin became famous all over the UK for Perks and Llewellyn lavender which won international awards for 150 years. Its popularity waned when new kid on the block - Eau de Cologne - became fashionable. During the vandalisation of the town in 1961 Miss Lewis the pharmacist at Perks and Llewellyn saved the Victorian interior of the late Georgian chemist shop in the High Street (replaced by the present ghastly Woolworth's) with its fixtures, fittings and contents. It can be seen in all its glory in Hitchin Museum. Among exhibits are the poison book, apothecary jars and lavender products. Today, thanks to Zoe and Alec Hunter of Cadwell Farm Ickleford, lavender once again is being grown. Miles of it can be enjoyed from the footpaths. Using the same method as Perks and Llewellyn oil is made by distilling. Products include soap, body lotion and lavender oil. Go and buy some.

Cadwell Farm: Ickleford

Market Theatre
The Only One of its Kind in the World
(even though it's in Sun Street and nowhere near the market but hey!)

In 1996, with West End theatre so expensive and so far away, Kirk Foster decided he would give Hitchin its very own "luvvies". Mind you, talk about lights and bushels; you do have to look for this little gem. It's hidden behind 6 Sun Street. He and his band of merry men and women transformed a derelict dump into a bijou 68 seat theatre. Bijou in that it measures 16 x 24 x 8 foot. Not a misprint. In the first year 402 trooped tentatively through the door, twelve years on, 12,500 beat a path. The theatre gets no handouts, Arts Council grants, annual funding or freebies. Comedies (*Marry Me or Be Evicted* a wonderful title) farces, histories, whodunits, scareys and thrillers – 124 so far with nairy a repeat – just one hour long are written by one man. Not a misprint. Kirk. His adult pantos are legendary. You get what you see in the title. *Puss and Dick, Slapper Beauty, The Emperor's Newd Clothes, Beauty and the Big Beastie, Peter Panties and Windy* are everything a panto should be. Un PC, lewd, rude, ham acting, the lot. Not for the faint hearted and don't sit in the front row. Have a drink in The Long Bar, a wonderful watering hole. During the summer, in the courtyard, the Company perform the only live soap opera in the world. *Weekenders* runs for eight weeks with each fifteen minute episode more ridiculous than the last. In true actor manager Good Companions tradition, the boss tours his shows. With Southend, Swindon, High Wycombe and Hayes under his belt, he is clearly heading for world domination. The Boy Done Good.

The Market Theatre

Pevsner's Perambulations Re-visited
These are the times that make men weep (Thomas Paine)

The famous architectural historian Sir Nicholas Pevsner toured Hertfordshire in a 1933 Wolseley Hornet. When he came to Hitchin in 1953 he waxed lyrical about the town in *The Buildings of England: Hertfordshire:* 'Hitchin is, after St Albans, the most visually satisfying town in the county…There is indeed not a shop nor an office building in the centre of town which seriously jars especially nothing on a wrong scale…' Within twenty years of his writing that the town had been vandalised. The Churchgate Carbuncle would have given him a heart attack. Gone is the 'long terrace of eight chequer brick cottages', the yellow brick Congregational chapel with its 'giant pilasters and pediment' and 20-21 Bridge Street with overhangs into Queen Street. Don't bother to traipse down Wymondley Road looking for Fred Rowntree's 1906 Lavender Croft. It's yet another block of flats. Did Town Planners (sic) not read Pevsner before giving their blessing for the following to be demolished: Angel Vaults, Sun Street, where Henry VIII stayed (built in 1450 it had medieval and 16th-century timbering); 114 Bancroft (15th-century Town Hall with a unique panelled canopy); Three Horseshoes, High Street (Tudor); 21 Bridge Street (15th century); The Grange, Portmill Lane (part of a Georgian group); Perks and Llewelyn in High Street; Dog Public House Brand Street. Vandals got as far as Wilkinson's (originally Safeway) until, mercifully, came a recession which means Bancroft is still as Pevsner said 'one of the best streets in Hertfordshire'. After the horror, The Hitchin Society, Hitchin Forum, Keep Hitchin Special and the Hitchin Historical Society sprang up so that it can never happen again. Shutting the gate after the horse has bolted maybe but at least Hitchin is now in safe hands.

Hitchin Museum: The Chemist Shop

The Intriguing Case
Of the King of Pippins

This is not a story about fairy folk although thanks to Michael Clark who should be given the Freedom of Hitchin it has a fairy tale ending. The brought back from the dead Hitchin Pippin takes pride of place on the cover of his *Apples a field guide.* Michael, Hertfordshire born and bred, spent years tracing the birth, life and almost death of the Hitchin Pippin. First recorded in 1896 this creamy, sweet, juicy dessert apple, like the Dodo was thought extinct until this cartoonist, graphic designer, lecturer, naturalist and a volunteer warden at Tewin Orchard finally tracked it down the last known named tree. Ten years ago when he put notices in the press Angela and Martin Cook of Hitchin and Sheila and Michael Wadsworth of Ickleford invited him to inspect the very old apple trees in their gardens. The Cook's tree is 100 years old, the Wadsworth's is fifty. Another, 80 years old, was found in nearby Weston. They answered the right description but were they the missing Pippin trees? Listening to a talk by Michael on Radio 4 Gerald Rose phoned in from Kent to say he had a named Hitchin Pippin still bearing fruit. Brogdale in Faversham where the apple tree museum is – more reverently known as the National Fruit Collection - with Wisley and two other specialist nurseries now propagate the Hitchin Pippin so its future is secure. Apples, says Michael, do not breed true from their own pips, propagation is by grafting, so in the nick of time – apple trees only last 120 years – he managed to propagate from that particular tree. He gave two of the first grafts to Codicote Community Orchard (opposite the church) where they can be seen in all their spindly splendour.

Codicote Community Orchard

Festival

Hitchin Festival is held in July every year. Broadly arts based, acts can include anything from films, string quartets, choirs, literary lunches, jazz, talks, plays, poetry, guided walks, art exhibitions, picnics in Priory Park, lunchtime concerts in St.Mary's and the famous Rhythms of the World (ROTW). One year *Four Poofs and a Piano* turned up which may have something to do with the fact that Martha Ross, mother of Jonathan, lives here. ROTW was founded in 1992 as part of the Hitchin Festival by Hitchin Oxfam to raise funds. The first four years were held in Hitchin Town Hall before it spilled out into the streets. Hitchin's Glastonbury attracts artists from – well – all over the world including Siberia, Africa, South America, Tibet, India and of course, Hitchin. Acts include rock bands, performance art, circus acts, street performers, solo artists, big bands, jazz, buskers, the spoken word, mime, theatre and traditional folk to experimental techno stuff. Organised by volunteers ROTW is unique in the UK. Until recently it was the largest free festival of world music. Free because, like Mardi Gras in New Orleans and Carnival in Notting Hill, it was held in the streets. Sadly no longer. The music of the streets has been sanitised and is now held in the very proper Hitchin Priory grounds with nowhere near the same edgy atmosphere. In the old days ten stages with 140 acts and 800 performers took over the whole town. Who will forget the amazing Dreamcatcher, an artwork of epic proportions made from 15,000 plastic bags by children from local schools? ROTW, another of the many jewels in Hitchin's crown, takes place every summer over one weekend.

Rhythms of the World

The Radcliffe Road School Bell Mystery

Balm to the soul is Gainsford Court in Radcliffe Road. The old Victorian Church School complex has been sympathetically restored by David Kann Associates. The developer told the author that for some reason the bell on the original design was never installed. If this is true after a hundred and forty years it's come home. And very fine it looks too. Not that it will ever summon the little darlings to lessons; the last pupil went home in the 1950s. Ex-pupils however scotch the rumour saying that as the school bell was so much part of life in those days it is unimaginable it was not installed. Never mind, like all local myths and legends, it makes a good story. The school was the Gainsford Memorial Hall 1956- to 1977 and a Sikh temple from 1977-2006. Although Holy Saviour Church was designed by William Butterfield, he did not design the school or the almshouses known as The Cloisters. A builder whose name was - bizarrely – also William Butterfield - built the school to the designs of Revd. George Gainsford Senior incumbent of Holy Saviour. To add to the name confusion there were also two Revd. Gainsford's, father and son. The Cloisters were built in 1870 not by Butterfield the Builder but by George Warren. Butterfield or Warren no matter whoever designed them was clearly inspired by Butterfield the architect. Just to add to the general confusion bearing in mind the complex was C of E there is a building next to the school called St Bridget's. Turns out this was the old orphanage opened in 1873 also attached to Holy Saviour Church. Closed in 1933 it was taken over by the RC Holy Family Homes who in turn were wound up in 1955 and sold it in 1959.

Gainsford Court: Radcliffe Road

Market Square
The Jewel in Hitchin's Crown – well - one of them

Market Square is all that's left of a huge market which once stretched as far as Bancroft but Hitchin still has the largest open market in the Home Counties. In 1953 Pevsner wrote: *The town has… a real market square (rare in the county)* and there's still something very special about it. The last market held in the square was 1939. It moved to its present site in Churchyard in 1972. No-one knows when the market began but as Hitchin was a Royal Manor and market tolls went to the Crown it must have been early. The grain market was certainly here in the 1200s. Corn was still the chief product in 1912. Traders sold corn, barley, wheat and livestock to middle men who sold them on to traders in London. In 1720 Daniel Defoe commented on the large number of carriages bringing wheat into Hitchin Market. Pie Powder Courts (from the French *pieds poudres* – dusty feet) were held to dish out summary justice on itinerants. The Baliol's were given a charter to hold Hitchin Fair on a Tuesday every year and Hitchin still has a market every Tuesday. Until 1829 a bell was rung to announce trading. In 1850 John Hawkins of Hawkins and Company went as legal adviser with Samuel Lucas to ask the Crown if they could lease the market. Permission granted they formed Hitchin Market Company which in 1852 built the Corn Exchange (closed 1970). The grand Italianate style building written up in the *London Illustrated News* was later used for badminton, suffragette rallies and ice skating. In 1941 it was a British Restaurant where Pamela Churchill, who lived in Ickleford, did her bit for the war effort. Today it is again a restaurant.

The Market Square: 2008